THE HISPANIC INFLUENCE IN THE UNITED STATES

LATINOS
IN AMERICAN HISTORY

OCTAVIANO LARRAZOLO

BY SUSAN ZANNOS

Mitchell Lane
PUBLISHERS

P.O. Box 196
Hockessin, Delaware 19707

THE HISPANIC INFLUENCE IN THE UNITED STATES

LATINOS
IN AMERICAN HISTORY

OTHER TITLES IN THE SERIES

Visit us on the web: www.mitchelllane.com
Comments? email us: mitchelllane@mitchelllane.com

THE HISPANIC INFLUENCE IN THE UNITED STATES

LATINOS

IN AMERICAN HISTORY

OCTAVIANO

LARRAZOLO

BY SUSAN ZANNOS

Printing   1   2   3   4   5   6   7   8   9

Library of Congress Cataloging-in-Publication Data

Zannos, Susan.
    Octaviano Larrazolo / by Susan Zannos.
       p. cm. — (Latinos in American history)
    Summary: Presents a biography of Octaviano Larrazolo, governor of New Mexico, and the first Hispanic to serve in the United States Senate.
    Includes bibliographical references and index.
    ISBN 1-58415-181-1 (lib. bdg.)
    1. Larrazolo, Octaviano Ambrosio, 1859-1930. 2. Governors—New Mexico—Biography. 3. Hispanic Americans—New Mexico—Biography. 4. New Mexico—Politics and government—1848-1950. [1. Larrazolo, Octaviano Ambrosio, 1859-1930. 2. Governors. 3. Mexican Americans—Biography.]   I. Title. II. Series.
F801.L3Z36 2002
978.9'052'092--dc21
[B]
                                                             2002011061

ABOUT THE AUTHOR: Susan Zannos has been a lifelong educator, having taught at all levels, from preschool to college, in Mexico, Greece, Italy, Russia, and Lithuania, as well as in the United States. She has published a mystery *Trust the Liar* (Walker and Co.) and *Human Types: Essence and the Enneagram* (Samuel Weiser). Her book, *Human Types*, was recently translated into Russian, and in 2003 Susan was invited to tour Russia and lecture about her book. Another book she wrote for young adults, *Careers in Education* (Mitchell Lane) was selected for the New York Public Library's "Books for the Teen Age 2003 List." She has written many books for children, including *Chester Carlson and the Development of Xerography* and *The Life and Times of Franz Joseph Haydn* (Mitchell Lane). When not traveling, Susan lives in the Sierra Foothills of Northern California.

PHOTO CREDITS: Cover: Library of Congress; p. 6 Hulton/Archive; p. 9 Hulton/Archive; p. 12 Hulton/Archive; p. 15 Hulton/Archive; p. 18 State Records Center Photograph Collection, courtesy New Mexico State Records Center & Archives, no. 8146; p. 24 Texas State Library & Archives Commission; p. 26 Texas State Library & Archives Commission; p. 28 Hulton/Archive; p. 30 Library of Congress; p. 36 Hulton/Archive

PUBLISHER'S NOTE: This story is based on the author's extensive research, which she believes to be accurate. Documentation of this research can be found on p. 45.

    The spelling of the names in this book follow the generally accepted usage of modern day. The spelling of Spanish names in English has evolved over time with no consistency. Many names have been anglicized and no longer use the accent marks or any Spanish grammar. Others have retained the Spanish grammar. Hence, we refer to Hernando de Soto as "de Soto," but Francisco Vásquez de Coronado as "Coronado." There are other variances as well. Some sources might spell Vásquez as Vazquez. For the most part, we have adapted the more widely recognized spellings.

CONTENTS

William H. Bonney, known as Billy the Kid, was one of the most famous outlaws of the American West. Billy moved to New Mexico with his mother in 1871. She died three years later, and 13-year-old Billy joined up with cattle rustlers and horse thieves. He began a series of killings at the age of 16. He died before he was 21, shot down by sheriff Pat Garrett. Outlaws like Billy the Kid convinced voters that New Mexico was a wild and lawless place that should not be granted statehood.

NEW MEXICO

CHAPTER 1

BECOMES A STATE

Since 1848 when the signing of the Treaty of Guadalupe Hidalgo ended the war between the United States and Mexico, the territory of New Mexico had a well-deserved reputation for being a wild and lawless land. In fact it was rumored that after the American Civil War, General Sherman suggested, "The United States ought to declare war on Mexico and make it take back New Mexico." By 1910, New Mexico's struggle for statehood had been going on for a long time. Five constitutional conventions had been held in New Mexico, but none of them had produced a document acceptable to the Congress and the President of the United States.

New Mexico *was* wild! Given its very long history (Santa Fe, founded by the Spanish in 1610, is the oldest capital city in the United States) and the explosive mixture of cultures that peopled it, New Mexico was bound to be an exciting place, full of strong contrasts and conflicts. The Spaniards came during the 16th century. The Native Americans—the Navajo, Hopi, Apache, and Zuni Indians—resented these arrogant intruders who tried to destroy their religions and force Christianity on them. In 1821, when Mexico declared its independence from Spain, trade with the United States began. Anglo merchants and traders made fortunes traveling the Santa Fe Trail from Missouri to sell goods to the New Mexicans.

Other English-speaking settlers came to farm, to search for silver and gold, or to graze cattle on eastern New Mexico's grass-lands. Cowboys, miners, gamblers, cattle rustlers, and outlaws filled the frontier towns. The legendary outlaw Billy the Kid, who claimed he had killed 21 men by the time he was 21 years old, typified the view people in the eastern United States had of the residents of New Mexico. Many Easterners believed that because New Mexico had so many citizens who spoke a different language and had a different culture, it shouldn't become a state. It took 62 long years as a territory before New Mexico became the 47th state of the United States.

In 1910, Congress passed the Enabling Act, and President Howard Taft signed it. This act provided that a constitutional convention should be held in New Mexico. The Democratic and Republican Parties both campaigned vigorously to have candidates elected to the convention. One man who worked hard to write and support the most important provisions in the Constitution of New Mexico was not even a delegate to the convention.

Octaviano Larrazolo was a lawyer who lived and practiced law in Las Vegas, New Mexico. He had been an active member of the Democratic Party for many years. The county he lived in was solidly Republican, however, so he was not elected as a member of the convention. Nonetheless, he worked hard with the delegates to convince them that they must safeguard the rights of Mexican Americans. The resulting constitution that was offered to the people for approval contained the following provisions:

> The right of any citizen of the state to vote, hold office, or sit upon juries, shall never be restricted, abridged or impaired on account of religion, race, language or color, or inability to speak, read or write the English or Spanish languages…

The Enabling Act, passed on June 10, 1910 during the presidency of Howard Taft (shown here), made it possible for the Arizona and New Mexico Territories to become states. Although many members of Congress and many citizens opposed statehood for these western territories, President Taft signed the act.

Children of Spanish descent in the state of New Mexico shall never be denied the right and privilege of admission and attendance in the public schools or other public institutions of the state, and they shall never be classed in separate schools, but shall forever enjoy perfect equality with other children in all public schools and educational institutions of the state...

For Octaviano Larrazolo, these provisions were central to his most deeply held principles: equality of opportunity for all. He was aware that segregation existed in some states, so many children did not have access to good schools. He was aware that many states had laws that prevented men from voting if they could not read and write English. It was a great irony that for his principles he was accused of being a racist who was attempting to secure favoritism for the Spanish-speaking citizens. He eventually was driven to renounce the Democratic Party because its members campaigned against adoption of the constitution as it had been written. He stood firm, although it meant losing life-long friends.

To understand what was at stake, we can compare the articles above with the following passage in the constitution of the State of Arizona that was written the same year. It provided that a person could not vote if "he is unable to read the constitution of the United States in the English language, in such manner as to show he is neither prompted nor reciting from memory."

Before New Mexico could be granted statehood, it was necessary for the citizens to vote in favor of the proposed constitution that their delegates had written. Many people opposed it, including members of the Democratic Party. Octaviano Larrazolo campaigned vigorously for the passage of the constitution. He realized that it was not perfect, but he felt so strongly about the provisions for equality of all citizens that he believed it should be adopted.

Larrazolo had a reputation throughout the Southwest for being a "silver-tongued orator." Never had he been more eloquent than he was in defending the new state constitution. In December 1910, while he was still a member of the Democratic Party, he addressed a party meeting in Santa Fe. A few days earlier, the Democrats had held a party convention at which resolutions were passed opposing ratification of the proposed constitution. In his speech, Octaviano Larrazolo carefully covered the strengths and weaknesses of the constitution, and then concluded by saying,

> You know I am in favor of the adoption of this constitution. . . . I do not believe that it is the duty of a citizen to surrender his conscience to any man or set of men, or to any party of any name. . . . Every native citizen must unite in supporting this constitution. Why? Because it secures to you people of New Mexico your rights—Every one of them; the rights also of your children and in such manner

that they can never be taken away. . . . Do not wait until you are put in the position of Arizona which in two years will be able to disenfranchise every Spanish-speaking citizen.

Even though he was speaking to members of the Democratic Party, which was determined to oppose the constitution, his speech was greeted with applause and cheers. This speech was typical of the addresses he gave throughout the territory. He spoke in both English and Spanish. His son Paul recalled in his biography of his father, "He used magnificent English, and to hear him speak in his native Spanish language was plainly a pure delight."

The voting was held on January 12, 1911. There were nearly 32,000 votes in favor of the constitution and only 13,400 votes against it.

New Mexico and Arizona were both granted statehood in 1912, New Mexico with the only constitution of any state that guaranteed its citizens full rights no matter what language they spoke, what religion they practiced, or what color their skin happened to be. (The provisions in the laws of Arizona remained until 1970 when an Act of Congress prohibited such practices in the elective processes of any state.)

Although it cost him his membership in the political party he had supported for 30 years, Larrazolo was well satisfied with what had been achieved for the future of the citizens of New Mexico.■

Born to a family of pureblooded Zapotec Indians in a mountain village in Oaxaca, Mexico, Benito Juárez led his countrymen through the revolution. After winning the battle of La Reforma, the reform movement, Juárez became President of Mexico. Many wealthy landowners, military officers, and priests were angry with the Ley Juárez, the law of Juárez, which made all Mexicans equal before the law. Others, like the Larrazolo family, supported Juárez and fought for his liberal policies.

NEW NATIONS

During the 1800s, new nations were being born on the North American continent. Like any births, these were occasions of labor and great struggle. These struggles took the form of revolutions, civil wars, and battles over borders. To each of two great nations in their infancy, the United States and Mexico, a great leader with high principles and great dedication appeared to guide them. Both leaders came from backgrounds of poverty and labor to become presidents. Both attempted to create a legacy of humane and liberal laws. Both met with brutal opposition.

In the United States, Abraham Lincoln came from a poor family of frontiersmen and farmers to achieve the seemingly impossible task of abolishing slavery and preserving the Union. In Mexico, Benito Juárez came from a family of pure-blooded Zapotec Indians, sheepherders in the mountains of the southern state of Oaxaca, to lead his country through revolutions and invasions. Those who came after, who were inspired by the courage and the vision of these great men, who undertook to live by principle and moral strength no matter what the cost, also had their parts to play in the forming of these nations.

One such man, Octaviano Larrazolo, was born on December 7, 1859, in El Valle de San Bartolomé (later known as El Valle de Allende), Chihuahua, Mexico. His father, also named Octaviano Larrazolo, was a wealthy landowner and the father of five sons with his first wife, who had died. His grandfather, José Maria Larrazolo, had been a successful businessman in town; he died before young Octaviano was born. His mother, Donaciana Corral de Larrazolo, was his father's second wife. She was well educated and came from a distinguished family in southern Chihuahua.

Octaviano's early childhood was comfortable and peaceful in the Larrazolos' large home. True, friends who came to visit talked long into the night about the turmoil and battles that were taking place to the south. By the first of January in 1861, the army of Juárez had won the battle of La Reforma, the reform movement. After years of exile, suffering, and civil war, Benito Juárez rode into Mexico City in his black carriage and took the office of president. The landowners in Chihuahua were divided. Some, like Octaviano's parents and stepbrothers, had great respect for Juárez. Others were angry over the Ley Juárez, the law of Juárez, which made all Mexicans equal before the law. Many of the wealthy men and the priests and military officers who had had special privileges did not want to be equal.

Other reform laws followed: One law limited the property that could be owned by the Catholic Church. Another law abolished both slavery and all titles of nobility and gave all adult males the right to vote. These laws became part of the Mexican Constitution in 1857. Opposition to the constitution had been violent and plunged the country into three years of the Reform War. But now the war was over, and the Larrazolos and other liberals hoped that there would be peace and that Juárez would be able to govern the country wisely, as he had done with the state of Oaxaca when he was governor there.

That was not to be. Spain, England, and France invaded Mexico, saying that they wanted to be paid the money Mexico owed them. Juárez appealed to the United States for help, but while President Lincoln felt sympathy, he could do nothing because the American Civil War had just begun. President Juárez was able to negotiate with England and Spain, who agreed to wait for payment of the debt, and their soldiers returned home. However, Napoléon III of France was eager to create a French colony in the New World. In April 1862, France invaded Mexico with more troops. By 1863, thirty thousand French soldiers had captured Mexico City. In 1864 the Archduke Maximilian arrived to become the Emperor of Mexico under the protection of Napoléon.

Juárez, in his black carriage that came to be called "the government on wheels," moved his army north, with the French

In 1862, French troops sent by Louis Napoléon (shown here), President of France, invaded Mexico and began four years of fighting against the forces of Mexican president Benito Juárez. In 1864, Napoléon III sent Archduke Maximilian and proclaimed him Emperor of Mexico. By 1867 the French were defeated and Maximilian was executed.

troops in pursuit. Octaviano's father and stepbrothers joined Juárez's Army of the Republic and moved the family to the larger town of Parral in the state of Chihuahua, thinking they would be safer there. One day when the family had gathered for their noon meal, they heard cannons. Parral was under siege by French forces. Octaviano, who was between four and five years old, watched the battle.

The Larrazolos returned to their family home in El Valle de Allende. It was a large structure of the Old Spanish style, located near the church. The French troops took it over for their head-quarters, leaving the family only one room, where Octaviano lived with his mother and two aunts. His father and brothers were off fighting with Juárez's army. Too young to appreciate the significance of these events, the boy soon became a favorite of the French soldiers, who often shared their meals with him.

Meanwhile, in the United States, the Civil War ended in 1865, but President Lincoln was assassinated before he wit-nessed the withdrawal of Napoléon's troops from Mexico. Juárez regained control of the government of Mexico. In Allende the departure of the French left the Larrazolo family in financial ruin, the house nearly destroyed, the land ravaged, the horses and other animals appropriated for the retreating army.

Octaviano's mother taught him how to read and write. He started school but did not like the teacher, who was a strict disci-plinarian. One day the teacher gave the boy a beating, and Octaviano refused to go back to school. By this time he had two younger brothers, Manuel and José, and the family lived in pov-erty. His parents knew Octaviano was intelligent and capable, but he had few prospects for education under the existing cir-cumstances. His father spoke with their parish priest, a good friend, about the boy.

Very suddenly, when he was 10 years old, nearly 11, Octaviano's life changed completely. On the afternoon of No-vember 20, 1870, Octaviano was playing in the town plaza with other children when a man came and told him the priest wanted to see him. When he got to the parish house, the priest said the bishop of Arizona, John Salpointe, wanted to talk to him. What the bishop had to say astonished the boy. After a long talk, Salpointe asked him if he would like to go with him to the United States, where he would have the opportunity for an education.

The boy was in emotional turmoil. Even as young as he was, he was excited by the prospect of a world of opportunities, of travel, of education that was not available in his little town. But everything and everyone he knew and loved was in that little town—his parents, his brothers, his friends. He would be leaving everything familiar to go off with a complete stranger. Octaviano ran home to talk to his parents. He found his mother crying—his father had been talking to her about their eldest son's opportunity. Although torn by conflicting emotions, Octaviano and his parents agreed that he would go with Bishop Salpointe. They would leave the next day.

The whole family set to work preparing for his trip. Early the following morning the boy had clean clothes packed. One of his stepbrothers saddled the pony that a family friend had given them for the boy's journey. Later, in his unfinished memoirs, Octaviano recalled, "When I was dressed, my mother took me by the hand and we went to church. There, bathed in tears, at the altar of the Blessed Virgin, she turned me over in her prayers to the Mother of God and commended me to her care and protection in my pilgrimage in foreign lands." They returned home and had breakfast with the entire family. Then his father took him to the parish house, where the bishop and a priest who was traveling with him were waiting.

Before he left, his father took him aside and said, "You are taking with you to a foreign country the good name which I have given you. Always keep it that way."

The boy climbed into the bishop's carriage, and the journey began.

After leaving Mexico when he was 10 years old and traveling with Bishop Salpointe of Tucson, Octaviano Larrazolo attended St. Michael's College near Santa Fe, New Mexico. His career began in San Elizaro, in El Paso County, Texas, where he began teaching while studying at night to become a lawyer.

JOURNEYS

At that time journeys were measured in months as well as in miles. On November 21, 1870, ten-year-old Octaviano Larrazolo set off with Bishop Salpointe and Father Bernal in the bishop's carriage. Their destination, Tucson, Arizona, was 700 miles away across deserts, plateaus, grasslands, and mountains. The first leg of their trip took them north through the state of Chihuahua to Chihuahua City, the largest city Octaviano had seen so far in his brief life. They stopped there awhile before heading on to the north.

The days were warm, but the farther north they went, the colder the nights became. Sometimes they reached small settlements where they were given shelter. More often night found them alone in the vast empty land, with the brilliant stars spread across the deep desert sky above. They slept wrapped in blankets under the carriage. The two priests began teaching Octaviano English, and they taught him how to assist them at the daily mass they celebrated. It took them many days to reach the town that is now named Ciudad Juárez, where they crossed the Rio Grande to the town that is now El Paso. At that time El Paso was only a few scattered adobe houses. The three travelers did not stop there but continued northward, following the Rio Grande to Las Cruces in New Mexico Territory. They were now in Bishop Salpointe's diocese, and they rested a few days at the home of the parish priest.

By this time the boy was well aware of the respect and affection that people felt toward his protector. John Salpointe had come to the United States from France as a missionary. He cared deeply about the Indian people and continued to visit them even after he became bishop of Arizona. His diocese was enormous, and thinly populated. He traveled constantly from Texas to the California border. The villages were small and poor and were able to offer very little support for their bishop.

In the unfinished memoirs Octaviano Larrazolo wrote later, he described the life of Salpointe:

> I happen to know that he did not receive one dollar from the priests in the diocese. Instead of that he distributed the small income that was sent to him by the organization known as the Propagation of the Faith, in France. He received $5,000 a year from them. This money he would divide among his priests in the diocese and the balance he gave to the good sisters to help them along in their schoolwork. So it was that he himself always lived in utter poverty and privation. . . . His principal food was beans and other vegetables that he raised himself in the summertime. It was a good thing that he wore a presentable cassock which made him appear decently dressed, because under that cassock there was very little else, and that little rather unpresentable. How well do I remember that often on Saturday evening he used to call me, "Octaviano, look among the old clothes and see if you can find a shirt that I can wear." I would patiently look, finally I would succeed in finding an old shirt with half a dozen or more holes in it. . . . He would wear it on Sunday morning. That man was a true apostle and certainly a man of God. Such was the life he led as long as I was with him.

It was early January of 1871 before the bishop, the priest, and Octaviano (now 11 years old) began traveling west from Las Cruces, New Mexico, on their way to Tucson. As they entered the Arizona Territory, they saw the Chiricahua Mountains ahead of them, rugged and beautiful. The Apache Indians in that area were fighting for the land they considered their own. While the party camped in the mountains, they became aware that Indians surrounded them. They could not see them, but they could hear the sounds of their horses. When they hitched up the carriage and started out, the bishop walked ahead, counting his rosary beads. Octaviano could hear the Indians, but their party was not disturbed. In later years Octaviano had frequent opportunities to see the relationship the bishop had with the Indians. Often Indians would come to where Salpointe was camped to welcome him. One old chief told him, "Be not afraid of Indian while you travel. Travel without fear. Indian takes care of you." Octaviano remembered that first journey to Tucson, and the Indians he had heard but never seen.

Octaviano began going to the small school that the bishop had started in Tucson. By 1873 he wrote to his father that he had started school in Las Cruces, where he had many classmates and was living with the local priest. He went to that school for about two years, until a flood destroyed the buildings in 1875. Then he traveled north to Santa Fe. He was nearly 16 years old, and Bishop Salpointe enrolled him as a boarder at St. Michael's College.

Saint Michael's consisted of two adobe buildings standing near the San Miguel Church, where the boys attended church services every day. The course of study included English grammar and composition, Spanish, elocution (public speaking), arithmetic, algebra and geometry, U.S. history, vocal music, and chemistry. The practical skills of typing and bookkeeping were also taught. There were no separate grades, and each boy was instructed and tested according to his level of learning. An intelligent and eager student like Octaviano was able to get a good education.

After two years of study at Saint Michael's College, Octaviano faced a difficult decision. Should he become a priest? During the years he had lived and traveled with Bishop Salpointe, visiting the priests in their parishes in little Southwest villages, assisting with the celebration of mass every day, he thought he wanted to be a priest. Now he wasn't sure. He was a serious young man with a strong sense of duty. The problem was that he wasn't sure where his duty lay. He had confidence in his abilities—he was successful in his studies; he was already recognized for his speaking abilities in both Spanish and English; he had proven his courage in many dangerous situations. He had also grown to be a handsome young man, nearly six feet tall, slender but strong and healthy. He thought that he could succeed at whatever he chose to do. But he didn't know what to choose.

Octaviano left Santa Fe and traveled back to Tucson to consult with the kind old man who had been both father and mother to him since he was 10 years old. It was 1877, and Bishop Salpointe asked Octaviano to make one last trip with him to visit some of the parishes in his diocese. They traveled east through New Mexico on the road that had brought them to Tucson seven years before, visiting the priest in San Elizaro, which was then the county seat of El Paso County. By the time they got back to Tucson, Octaviano had made his decision. He knew from letters that his family's situation was very bad, and that they needed help. Three more children, two brothers and a sister, had been born since he left home, and the family was living in desperate poverty.

He had thoughts of returning to Mexico, but he knew that there was little he would be able to do to earn a living there. He decided to go to San Elizaro, where it seemed there were many opportunities for work. In addition, it was near the border between Texas and Chihuahua, which would make visiting his family easier. Octaviano moved to San Elizaro in 1878 and presented the high recommendations he had received from Bishop Salpointe and from St. Michael's College. He soon got a job teaching in the public school. He also began farming, and with the proceeds of his first harvest was able to buy a house. The following year his parents and the three young children—Juan, who was six; José, four; and Refugio, two—arrived in San Elizaro. After nine years the family was together again, living with Octaviano. His youthful journeys were over. ■

Arrogant, extravagant, and corrupt, Antonio López de Santa Anna often changed sides in battle and in politics, depending on who was winning. In 1831, after claiming victory over Spanish forces at Tampico, Santa Anna became President of Mexico. In February of 1836, he led forces that attacked the fort at the Alamo, Texas, and massacred the 187 brave men defending it.

RESPONSIBILITIES

Octaviano made many friends in his new community, among them Don Jesus Cobos and his lovely daughter, Rosalia. Octaviano dated her, and they were married on April 25, 1881. By this time the young husband was a school administrator as well as a teacher, since he had been appointed a member of the board of examiners for schools. He continued farming because the family needed the extra income. His father died a year after the young couple married. His mother and the three children continued to live with him and Rosalia. The young couple had their first child, a son they named Juan Bautista, in February 1883.

With his mother, his wife, three siblings, and a baby to support, Octaviano knew he had to make more money. He decided that he would become a lawyer. Obviously he could not go off to law school, so after long days of teaching, farming, and doing the chores at home, he studied law at night by the light of a coal lamp. Local attorneys and judges encouraged him and helped him in his studies. The more he learned about the legal system of the United States, the more respect he developed for the American form of government. On December 11, 1884, in the

"Be always sure you are right, then go ahead," was Davy Crockett's motto. A hunter and Indian fighter, Crockett was nationally known as a hero and a political representative of the frontier in the Congress of the United States. When he was 49 years old, Davy Crockett died a hero's death at the Alamo, helping Texas win independence from Mexico.

District Court of El Paso County, Octaviano Larrazolo became an American citizen.

Texas was a good place to learn about the laws of his new country. After a long and eventful history, Texas had become a state in 1845. Like the rest of the southwestern part of North America, Texas had originally been explored by the Spanish, who set up missions beginning in 1682 in an attempt to convert the Indians to Christianity. When Mexico became independent from Spain in 1821, Texas was part of the Republic of Mexico. The Mexican government thought it would be a good idea to have more people live in Texas because more people would mean more taxes paid to the government. As it turned out, that wasn't a very good idea at all.

Land was offered for sale at 12 cents an acre, encouraging more and more English-speaking settlers to move to Texas from other states. New immigrants from Europe also came. As large numbers settled in Texas, there began to be problems with the Mexican government. The settlers didn't like the schools because they taught only Spanish. Many of the settlers had come from the southern states and brought slaves with them. They were angry because the Mexican government had outlawed slavery. The settlers wanted to make their own laws. They made so much trouble that in 1830 the Mexican government said that no more Americans could settle in Texas.

In 1833 the settlers, led by Stephen Austin, sent an official list of their complaints to the Mexican government. That same year General Antonio López de Santa Anna, an arrogant and aristocratic leader, became president of Mexico. He soon became dictator as well. The American settlers were ready to fight for their independence, and Santa Anna's troops marched north to stop them. On February 23, 1836, a group of less than 200 Texas rebels, including such famous frontiersmen as Davy Crockett and Jim Bowie, were trapped inside the Alamo fort by 4,000 Mexican soldiers. The Texans held out for 13 days. When they ran out of ammunition, Mexican troops stormed the Alamo, killing all the defenders.

The massacre at the Alamo enraged the settlers in Texas. "Remember the Alamo!" became their battle cry. General Sam Houston gathered all the Americans who wanted to fight. Though outnumbered, they defeated Santa Anna's army in the Battle of San Jacinto and captured Santa Anna himself. They had won the war.

The new Republic of Texas had a lot of problems. In 1845 the Texas legislature decided that Texas should join the United States. The United States wasn't sure they wanted Texas. For

After choosing to spend much of his youth with the Cherokee Indians in Tennessee, Sam Houston enlisted to fight England in the War of 1812. He later moved to Texas where he was elected commander-in-chief of the armies. After the fall of the Alamo in 1836, he defeated Santa Anna's forces in the Battle of San Jacinto and secured the independence of Texas.

one thing, the Northern states didn't want another state that had slavery. For another, they were afraid that if Texas became a state, it would cause a war with Mexico.

They were right. Texas became the 28th state on December 29, 1845. In 1846 the U.S.-Mexico War started over the boundaries between Texas and Mexico. Once again Mexico brought calamity upon itself: in the peace treaty that Mexico was forced to sign in 1848, the United States gained the whole northern half of Mexico. This is the area that is now the states of Texas, Arizona, Nevada, California, Utah, and New Mexico. At that time they were still territories.

Texas had been a state for 40 years when two of the judges who had been helping Octaviano Larrazolo appointed him chief clerk of the U.S. district court at El Paso, Texas. Octaviano had been a citizen for only three months. He became familiar with court procedures and records, and he associated constantly with lawyers and with people about their legal problems. He earned more money than he had in the schools, but he also had more obligations: his second son was born in 1885.

Octaviano was very active in the business and political life of El Paso County. He moved his family to the town of El Paso, which had grown rapidly once the Southern Pacific Railroad was completed in 1883. He was twice elected to the office of clerk of the district court (which was an elective office, unlike the federal appointment he had previously). He passed the legal exams and was admitted to practice law in Texas. In 1890 he was elected district attorney.

Then tragedy struck. In 1891 Octaviano's wife died giving birth to a baby girl, who was named after her mother, Rosalia. Octaviano's life changed dramatically in the next few years. In 1892 he married Maria Garcia, the young daughter and only child of friends in San Elizaro. Maria had just graduated from high school. The following year his mother died, after living with him for the 14 years since they had been reunited. His brothers and sister were now on their own—he had raised them successfully. Even though he was a prominent lawyer and politician in El Paso, he was ready for a change.

Octaviano still had many friends in New Mexico Territory. They urged him to move there to share the opportunities and challenges. His oldest son, Juan, was already in school at St. Michael's in Santa Fe, the boarding school that Octaviano had attended. In 1895 Octaviano and Maria moved their family to New Mexico. They chose the town of Las Vegas for their home. It was probably the largest town in New Mexico at that time, and a center of commerce. It seemed the best place to begin a new life. ■

In 1900, 1906, and 1908, Octaviano Larrazolo ran for congress on the Democratic ticket in New Mexico. During these campaigns he was accused of racism for insisting that Spanish-speaking citizens of New Mexico should have the same rights as English-speaking citizens.

POLITICS

In all ways but one, his new home in Las Vegas, New Mexico, suited Octaviano Larrazolo very well. He had many old friends there from his days traveling with Bishop Salpointe and attending school in nearby Santa Fe. And he soon made many new friends. He opened his law practice in a building by the Old Town Plaza and soon was one of the most successful lawyers in the territory. He purchased a home not far from the Catholic church and the courthouse—the two places to which he was most attached.

By the beginning of the 20th century, Larrazolo was very well known in New Mexico. In those days movies were in their infancy, and there was no television or radio. Court trials, particularly trials with juries, were a form of entertainment for the public. People loved to hear the successful lawyers present their cases. Octaviano was known as the "silver-tongued orator" and had many fans, just as movie stars do today. In the northern counties where many of the jurors and witnesses did not speak English, he would perform in both Spanish and English, to the delight of the crowds. His wide reputation as a lawyer helped his political effectiveness.

The only real difficulty was the political situation in New Mexico Territory. Larrazolo had learned about political processes in Texas, where he was a Democrat. He became active in the Democratic Party in his new home. The year after he arrived, he supported the Democratic candidate to Congress by traveling throughout the northern part of the territory making speeches. Four years later he himself was the Democratic candidate.

He needed all the help he could get, because the Democratic Party in New Mexico was much weaker than the Republican Party, which was particularly strong in Larrazolo's San Miguel County. Even though he campaigned hard in 1900 to be elected to Congress, he was defeated. He came home and continued his practice of law. He also wrote articles for a Spanish newspaper.

He wrote and made speeches about the need for a stronger educational system in the territory. His own experience teaching school in Texas gave him a solid foundation in effective class-room methods for bilingual teaching. He knew that it was impor-tant to use Spanish in teaching English to Spanish-speaking children. And he stressed the necessity of English-speaking children to learn Spanish because of the importance of interna-tional trade with Mexico and the countries of Central and South America. These ideas were not popular at that time.

In 1906 the Democratic Party again asked Octaviano Larrazolo to run for the U.S. Congress from the Territory of New Mexico. Again he agreed. Again he campaigned hard, and again he lost. This time he lost by a very narrow margin, only 226 votes, and there was reason to believe that there had been irregu-lar voting practices. The Democrats challenged the election on grounds of voting fraud. But the congressional committee that was responsible for evaluating such charges did not act until it was nearly time for the 1908 election. Larrazolo ran again, and again lost by only a very few votes.

During these election campaigns, Octaviano was accused of racism, of supporting educational reforms and other measures that would place the Spanish-speaking native population in positions of power. He was outraged by these accusations. The principles that he supported had always been that of equal opportunity for all citizens. Furthermore, he had witnessed the prejudice of the English-speaking settlers against the native residents. He had not introduced the issue of race. He had attempted to bring an existing situation into the light of public discussion.

Larrazolo felt that his defeat in the elections of 1906 and 1908 occurred because many Democrats would not vote for him because he was Mexican American. He was angry with the Democratic Party because they did not actively contest the election—in fact, the Democratic members of the committee to investigate the charges of fraud didn't even show up. Despite his displeasure with the party he had supported for 30 years, he campaigned actively and effectively in support of the state constitution. He had seen that many liberal provisions for the protection of Spanish-speaking citizens had been included in the constitution.

After the constitution had been ratified, Octaviano resigned from the Democratic Party. In August 1911, he wrote a long letter to the chairman of the Territorial Central Committee explaining his action. In his letter, which was well documented, he pointed out that while the Democrats had 26 members at the constitutional convention, not one was Hispanic. The Republicans, on the other hand, sent members representing "all elements of our mixed population."

Larrazolo went on to say that these facts and many others "have forced me to the humiliating conviction that in the Democratic party of New Mexico, there exists an element of intolerance that should not be countenanced or encouraged . . . it has marked the end of my period of usefulness to our citizenship as a member of that party."

In the years following his departure from the Democratic Party, Larrazolo was busy with his law practice and his large family. In addition to the three children from Octaviano's first marriage and their son Octaviano Jr., who had been born before they left Texas, he and Maria had eight more children, six boys and two girls. The Larrazolos outgrew their first house and bought a larger one. As his older sons from his first marriage grew up and married and had children, they became frequent visitors. Fortunately Maria's parents had moved to New Mexico to be near their only daughter and their grandchildren, so Maria's mother was able to help care for the children.

About 1910 Larrazolo bought a small ranch in the valley of the Mora River. In the summer Maria would stay there with her parents and the children, and sometimes the grandchildren would come too. Larrazolo would go to the ranch on weekends. On one such trip in early September, he was caught in an unexpected snowstorm while driving his horse and buggy toward the ranch. The snow kept falling harder and harder until he could no longer see the road. He got down from the buggy and attempted to lead the horse, but the horse had a different opinion about which direction they should take. Finally it became dark and they were completely lost. Octaviano climbed back into the buggy and let the horse go wherever it wanted—it turned completely around and went the opposite direction. Before long Octaviano saw the lights of the ranch house and heard the shouts of his worried family. He was so stiff with the cold that the older boys had to lift him from the buggy. The horse had saved his life.

In Las Vegas the lawyers and doctors each formed a baseball team and competed with each other for recreation. In one of these hotly contended games, Larrazolo got to first base on a hit and then tried to steal second. Sliding into the base, he broke his leg. To make matters worse, the umpire called him out. He had to be carried off the field, and he appeared for his court cases on crutches for a while.

Despite snowstorms and broken legs on top of the heavy duties of supporting a large active family by a busy law practice, Octaviano Larrazolo also remained active by traveling through the central and northern counties of the state in his efforts to get equal representation for Spanish-speaking people. By 1914 his efforts were paying off with both parties. Benigno Hernandez was elected to the U.S. House of Representatives as a Republican. In 1916, Ezequiel Cabeza de Baca, a Democrat, was elected governor of New Mexico. Unfortunately he was very ill and died shortly after taking office.

In April 1917, the United States entered World War I by declaring war on Germany. Octaviano Jr., who had been studying at the University of Notre Dame, enlisted in the army and within a few months was fighting in France. The next oldest son, Carlos, was in a preparatory school in Washington, D.C., and planning to enter the U.S. Naval Academy. The next, Luis, was in the New Mexico Military Institute. The younger children were at home.

Nineteen-eighteen was a fateful year for the country and for the family. Ten-year-old Justiniano died in January. The grieving parents had heard nothing from Octaviano Jr. as the war in Europe was reaching its climax in the summer and fall. On the national scale, the Republican Party was preparing for the elections—control of the U.S. Senate was at stake, and the race in New Mexico was of national importance. The Republican senator, Albert B. Fall, and the leaders of the party felt that the candidate for governor of New Mexico should be Hispanic.

In July a committee of Republicans came to see Octaviano Larrazolo at this ranch. He had been ill, crushed by the grief over the death of his young son and his worry over the older boy in the army. The party leaders urged Octaviano to run for governor. It was a hard decision. He was 59 years old and in poor health. If he were elected, it would mean giving up his law practice and having to start all over again. He went back to Las Vegas and talked to Maria about it. He had never in his life avoided making an effort just because it was difficult, and this could be an opportunity to carry out the ideas and principles he had struggled so hard for. He told the committee that if the Republican convention nominated him, he would accept.■

After the victory of the allies in World War I, American president Woodrow Wilson (shown here) went to Paris to work on the Versailles Treaty, which contained the Covenant of the League of Nations. The Senate rejected it by seven votes. President Wilson made a national tour to gain support for the treaty. In New Mexico, the House of Representatives passed a resolution condemning the treaty. The governor of New Mexico, Octaviano Larrazolo, believed in the principles of the League of Nations. Larrazolo vetoed the resolution, angering his own party.

GOVERNOR

O ctaviano Larrazolo was the Republican candidate for governor of New Mexico in 1918. As was to be expected, his opponents criticized him for changing parties, and they brought up the old accusations that he favored Mexican Americans over Anglos and would "Mexicanize" the state. Because of the war effort, and because a serious influenza epidemic was ravaging the state, campaign activities were kept to a minimum. Instead of the usual speeches, Larrazolo wrote an open letter stating his position on the issues. He concluded the letter by saying, "If I am elected to the office of governor I shall put into practice the principles that I have defended and on account of which undoubtedly I have made many enemies. Those principles are: 'Equal rights and privileges for all citizens of New Mexico without regard to ancestry.'"

On November 5, 1918, Octaviano Larrazolo was elected as the first Republican governor of the State of New Mexico. When he was interviewed by the news media, he repeated his intentions: "It shall be my purpose and earnest endeavor to give equal protection and recognition to the various sections of our state, without partiality or discrimination, always endeavoring to accomplish the greatest good possible for the greatest number."

The new governor gave his inauguration speech in English, and then gave it in Spanish. He concluded his inaugural address by speaking directly to the young people in the audience, telling them that "in the land of stars and stripes there are no privileged classes, but that the avenues to place and distinction are open equally to you all." After the inauguration came the considerable task of moving his whole big family from Las Vegas to the executive mansion in Santa Fe.

As governor of New Mexico, Octaviano Larrazolo accomplished a lot. In the process he made nearly everyone angry about one thing or another. He stood by his principles and acted from his best understanding, no matter who opposed him. That is not to say that he ignored the traditional political appointments. When he was criticized for removing the warden of the state penitentiary, he replied in a letter to the El Paso *Herald:* "I am making appointments with a view to efficiency and good service. At the same time I am working to keep the party in power . . . a man who does not play politics in an office like mine . . . is a—well, a damned fool."

At first he was successful in dealing with the state legislature. They passed a child labor law restricting the kinds of employment children could have and not allowing children to work while school was in session. They made school attendance compulsory for children between 6 and 16. They raised teachers' pay. They established bilingual methods of teaching. These things were all solid achievements. On these matters and other issues, the governor and the legislature worked harmoniously and effectively together. Nonetheless, the people who believed that only English should be used in the schools were angry.

On another issue, however, there was disagreement between Larrazolo and the legislature. Senator Fall and other Republican senators were determined to destroy President Woodrow Wilson. They opposed Wilson's proposal that the United States join the League of Nations at the end of World War I. Senator Fall addressed the New Mexico House of Representatives, asking them to pass a resolution condemning the League. They did. Governor Larrazolo vetoed their resolution. He believed in the principles of the League of Nations and in the importance of international cooperation. He openly opposed the Republican leadership.

Larrazolo angered many in the mining industry when he declared martial law in McKinley and Colfax Counties, where miners were preparing to strike. He did this because he believed that the strikes were being organized by foreign elements— Austrians, Italians, and Greeks—working in the Gallup mines, and that these were socialist agitators. Nonetheless, he was accused of being against the interests of the workingman. Many of the miners were Mexican Americans.

This was not the last time he would oppose his own supporters. Early in 1920, during his second year as governor, the 19th Amendment to the Constitution of the United States required state action. This was the amendment that would give women the right to vote. Larrazolo asked the New Mexico legislature not only to ratify the 19th Amendment, but also to amend their state constitution to give women the right to vote as well. The Spanish-speaking citizens, exactly the voters who most strongly supported Larrazolo, were the ones most opposed to women's suffrage. It was against the customs and traditions of Mexican-American culture for women to participate in political action. By his support of women's right to vote, Larrazolo was once again defending his basic belief in equal opportunity for all citizens. He was also making a lot of Spanish-speaking voters angry.

Octaviano worked tirelessly for the good of New Mexico. Among the projects that he attempted was the effort to transfer federal lands to the control and ownership of the states. Greatly concerned about the need for more money to finance pressing state projects, he worked to establish a better system of taxation. One of his main concerns was the construction of good roads (perhaps he was remembering the long journeys he had taken as a young man with Bishop Salpointe). He also set up the first Public Health Department in New Mexico.

As his term of office drew to a close in 1920, the Republicans began coming out in open opposition to Larrazolo's policies. It was apparent that they intended to replace him as governor. They were not interested in an independent governor who worked for the greatest good of the most people. They wanted a governor who worked for the greatest good of the Republican Party. Although the nominating convention was a hard-fought struggle between Octaviano Larrazolo's supporters and the Republican Party bosses who wanted him out, the bosses won. Larrazolo, always the politician as well as the independent thinker and fighter, supported Merritt Mechem, the Republican candidate for governor who was elected to succeed him.

Octaviano Larrazolo was 62 years old. In poor health when he became governor, he had several periods of illness while in office. He still had four young children at home to care for, and his law practice in Las Vegas was gone. He was left with hardly any resources. He and his family moved again to El Paso, Texas, where he spent two years practicing law. He traveled frequently to Mexico, where he was working to strengthen trade relations with the United States.

By 1922, however, a movement had started among independent Republicans in New Mexico to convince Larrazolo to return to politics in that state. He did return, moving his family to a comfortable home in Albuquerque and practicing law there. By that time Albuquerque was the largest city in New Mexico, and Larrazolo once again had a thriving law practice—being the former governor didn't hurt at all. He also continued with his business interests in El Paso and his frequent trips to Mexico. And once again he was deeply involved with New Mexico politics, although he did not run for public office again until 1926. He served in the New Mexico House of Representatives in 1927 and 1928.

In the elections of 1928, Larrazolo agreed to run for a seat in the U.S. Senate, even though his doctors had told him not to. He was 69 years old, and his health was failing. Nonetheless, he ran and was elected. He was the first Mexican-born member of the

U.S. Senate, which is the highest political position that anyone not born in the United States can achieve.

He did not hold his Senate post long. In January 1929 his health broke down completely and his doctors ordered him home. Shortly after returning to Albuquerque, he suffered a severe stroke that left him paralyzed. He died on April 7, 1930, at the age of 70. Before his death he called his sons to his bedside. Remembering his father's words to him when he had left home 60 years before, he said to his boys, "I will not leave you much by way of worldly goods, as I possess very little. But I do have a good name which I have endeavored all my life to keep unblemished. Remember always to keep it that way." ■

CHRONOLOGY

1859 Octaviano Larrazolo Jr. born in Allende, Chihuahua, Mexico, on December 7

1860s Larrazolo family loses everything to French invasion force

1870 Salpointe, bishop of Arizona, takes Octaviano to Tucson

1875 moves with Salpointe to Santa Fe, New Mexico; enrolls in St. Michael's College

1877 returns to Tucson to teach for one year

1878 moves to San Elizaro in El Paso County, Texas, and teaches for five years

1879 his parents and three youngest siblings move in with him

1881 marries Rosalia Cobos

1882 father dies

1883 son Juan Bautista born

1884 becomes an American citizen

1885   joins the Texas Democratic Party and becomes chief clerk of the U.S. district court; son José Maria born

1888   admitted to the Texas bar

1890   elected district attorney

1891   wife Rosalia dies giving birth to daughter Rosalia

1892   marries Maria Garcia

1893   mother dies

1894   son Octaviano Jr. born

1895   moves to Las Vegas, New Mexico; daughter Josefina born

1897   son Carlos born

1900   son Luis Fernando born

1903   son Heliodoro born

1906   daughter Maria born; daughter Josefina dies

1908   son Justiniano born

1910   attends constitutional convention for New Mexican statehood; son Pablo (Paul) born

1911   switches to Republican Party

1913   son Rafael born

1918   son Justiniano dies; elected governor of New Mexico

1919   sends National Guard to break coal strikes; endorses 19th Amendment

1927, 1928   serves in the New Mexico House of Representatives

1928   becomes first Hispanic to serve in U.S. Senate

1930   dies in Albuquerque, New Mexico, on April 7

TIMELINE IN HISTORY

1610   Spanish found Santa Fe

1682   Spanish establish missions in Texas

1821   Mexico declares independence from Spain

1836   Texans massacred at the Alamo by General Santa Anna's soldiers

1845   Republic of Texas becomes the 28th state

1846   U.S.-Mexico War begins

1848   Treaty of Guadalupe Hidalgo ends the war between U.S. and Mexico; northern Mexico becomes U.S. territories of Texas, California, New Mexico, Arizona, Utah, and Nevada.

1849   California gold rush begins after gold is discovered at Sutter's Mill

1853   Gadsden Purchase of land by United States from Mexico increases Arizona and New Mexico Territories

1860   Abraham Lincoln is elected U.S. president

1861   American Civil War begins; Benito Juárez wins the war of La Reforma and becomes president of Mexico

1862   French invade Mexico

1865   American Civil War ends; Lincoln is assassinated

1883   Southern Pacific Railroad is completed

1891   the first movies are released; the first true automobile is made in France

1896   William McKinley is elected U.S. president

1898   Spanish-American War begins; it lasts over a year

1901   President McKinley is assassinated and Theodore Roosevelt becomes U.S. president

1908   William Howard Taft is elected U.S. president

1912   New Mexico and Arizona become the 47th and 48th states

1917   United States declares war against Germany and enters World War I

1919   World War I ends; President Woodrow Wilson proposes League of Nations

1920   the 19th Amendment is ratified, giving women the right to vote

1924   Albert B. Fall, Interior Secretary, is charged with conspiracy and fraud in Teapot Dome scandal

1925   John Logie Baird sends the first television transmission

1929   stock market crash brings the Great Depression to the United States

1933   Hitler becomes chancellor of Germany and his Nazis begin their terror

1939   World War II begins

1945   World War II ends

1946   the United Nations, which effectively replaces the League of Nations, holds its first meeting

FOR FURTHER READING

For Young Adults

Aylesworth, Thomas G., and Virginia L. Aylesworth. *The Southwest.* New York: Chelsea House Publishers, 1988.

Hanson-Harding, Alexandra. *Texas.* New York: Children's Press, 2001.

Herda, D. J. *Historical America: The Southwestern States.* Brookfield, Conn.: The Millbrook Press, 1993.

Kent, Deborah. *New Mexico.* New York: Children's Press, 1999.

McDaniel, Melissa. *Arizona.* New York: Benchmark Books, 2000.

Wepman, Dennis. *Benito Juárez.* New York: Chelsea House Publishers, 1986.

Works Consulted

Cordova, Alfred C., and Charles B. Judah. *Octaviano Larrazolo: A Political Portrait.* Albuquerque, N.M.: Division of Research, University of New Mexico, 1952.

Lamb, Ruth S. *Mexican Americans: Sons of the Southwest.* Claremont, Calif.: Ocelot Press, 1970.

Larrazolo, Paul F. *Octaviano A. Larrazolo: A Moment in New Mexico History.* New York: Carlton Press, Inc., 1986.

ON THE WEB

Handbook of Texas Online: Larrazolo, Octaviano Ambrosio
http://www.tsha.utexas.edu/handbook/online/articles/view/LL/fladc.html

Hispanic Americans in Congress—Larrazolo
http://www.loc.gov/rr/hispanic/congress/larrazolo.html

Larrazolo, Octaviano Ambrosio, American National Biography Online
http://www.anb.org/articles/06/06-00360-article.html

Larrazolo, Octaviano Ambrosio, 1859–1930, Congressional Biographical Directory
http://bioguide.congress.gov/scripts/biodisplay.pl?index=L000101

Octaviano A. Larrazolo Papers 1841–1981, Biography
http://elibrary.unm.edu/oanm/NmU/nmu1%23mss614bc/nmu1%23mss614bc_m1.html

GLOSSARY

Anglo (ANG-low)—an English-speaking person of European ancestry

appropriated (uh-PRO-pree-ayt-ud)—taken for one's own use with consent or the right to do so

articles (ART-uh-kuls)—specific sections in a legal document

assassinate (uh-SASS-uh-nayt)—to kill a public figure, usually a political or religious leader

bilingual (bye-LING-gwul)—able to speak two languages

bishop (BISH-up)—a member of the highest order in the Catholic Church

campaign (kam-PAYN)—an organized attempt to gain public support

candidate (KAN-duh-dayt)—a person who tries to be elected to public office